Octaves for the Viola

Book One

by Cassia Harvey

CHP241

©2014 by C. Harvey Publications All Rights Reserved.
6403 N. 6th Street
Philadelphia, PA 19126
www.charveypublications.com

Octaves for the Viola   1

Book One

By Cassia Harvey
Edited by Myanna Harvey

Oh, Susannah — Foster

©2014 C. Harvey Publications All Rights Reserved

2

Alborada — Rimsky-Korsakov

Octaves for the Viola, Book One

3

Simple Gifts — Trad.

©2014 C. Harvey Publications All Rights Reserved

4

Travelling Tune — Harvey

Octaves for the Viola, Book One

5

6

Taps — Butterfield

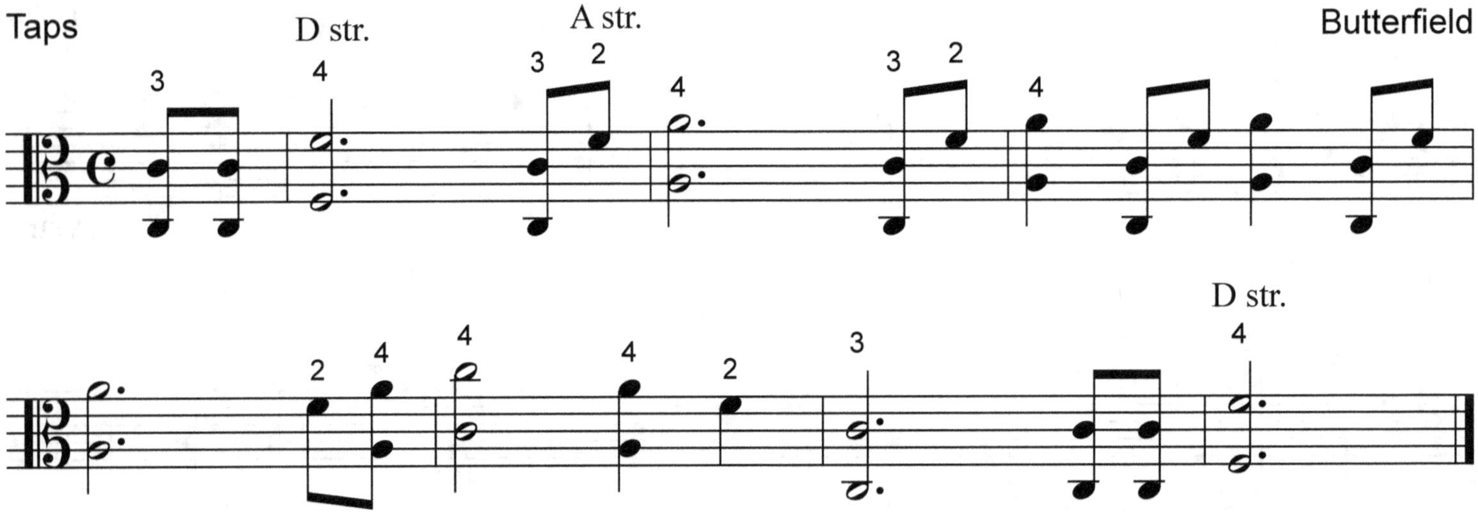

Octaves for the Viola, Book One

9

Quadrille — Trad.

Octaves for the Viola, Book One 11

11

The Blacksmith — Trad.

12

13

The Battle Cry of Freedom — Trad.

14

Across the Western Ocean — Trad.

16

Aiken Drum — Trad.

17

Old Joe Clark — Trad.

19

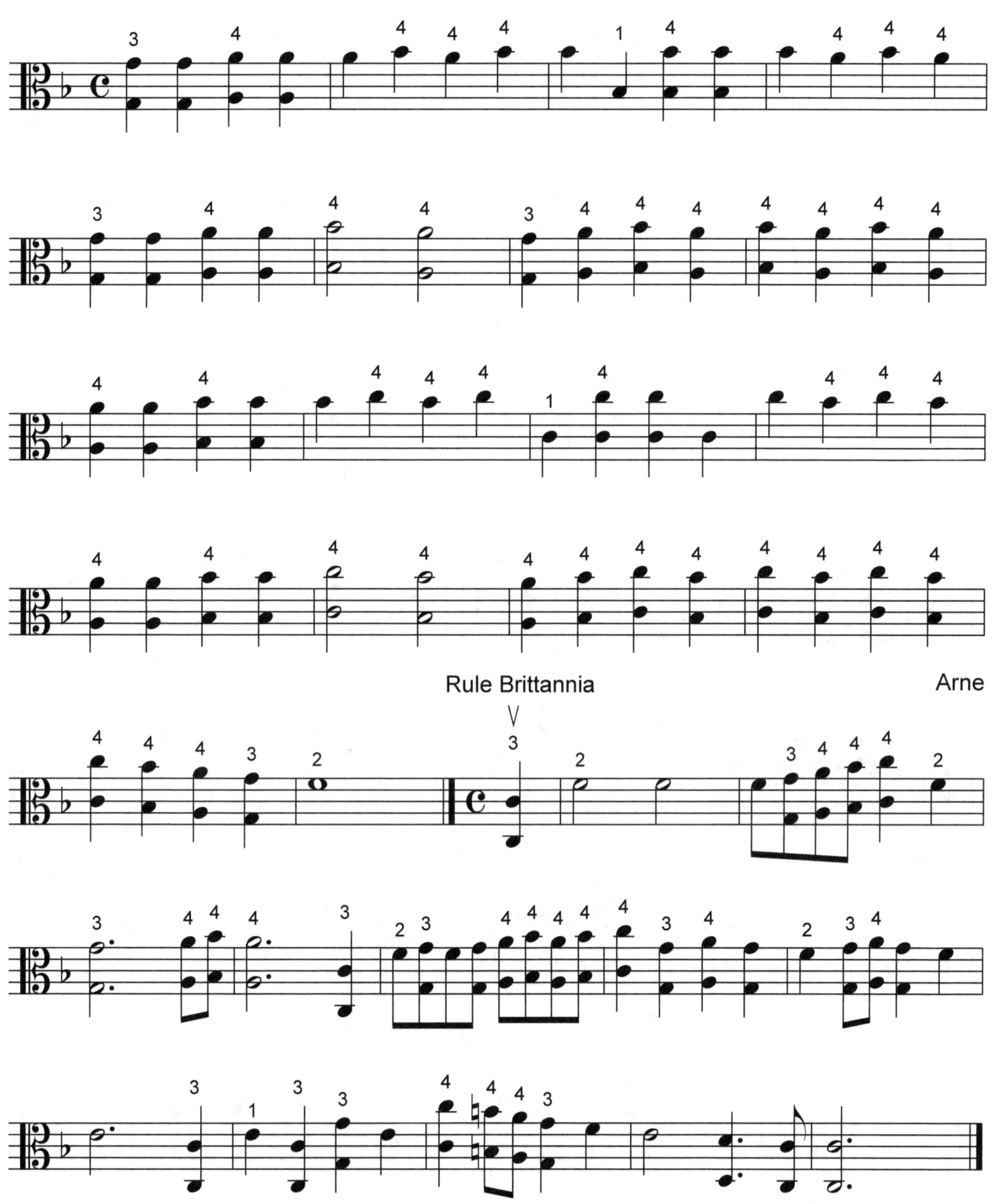

Rule Brittannia — Arne

20

Camptown Races — Foster

21

Lightly Row — Trad.

22

Ode to Joy — Beethoven

Octaves for the Viola, Book One

23

My Bonny Lies Over the Ocean — Trad.

25

Arkansas Traveler — Trad.

26

Danse Bacchanale — Saint-Saens

Octaves for the Viola, Book One

29

Blue-Eyed Girl
Trad.

30

Don Giovanni — Mozart

31

Country Gardens — Trad.

32

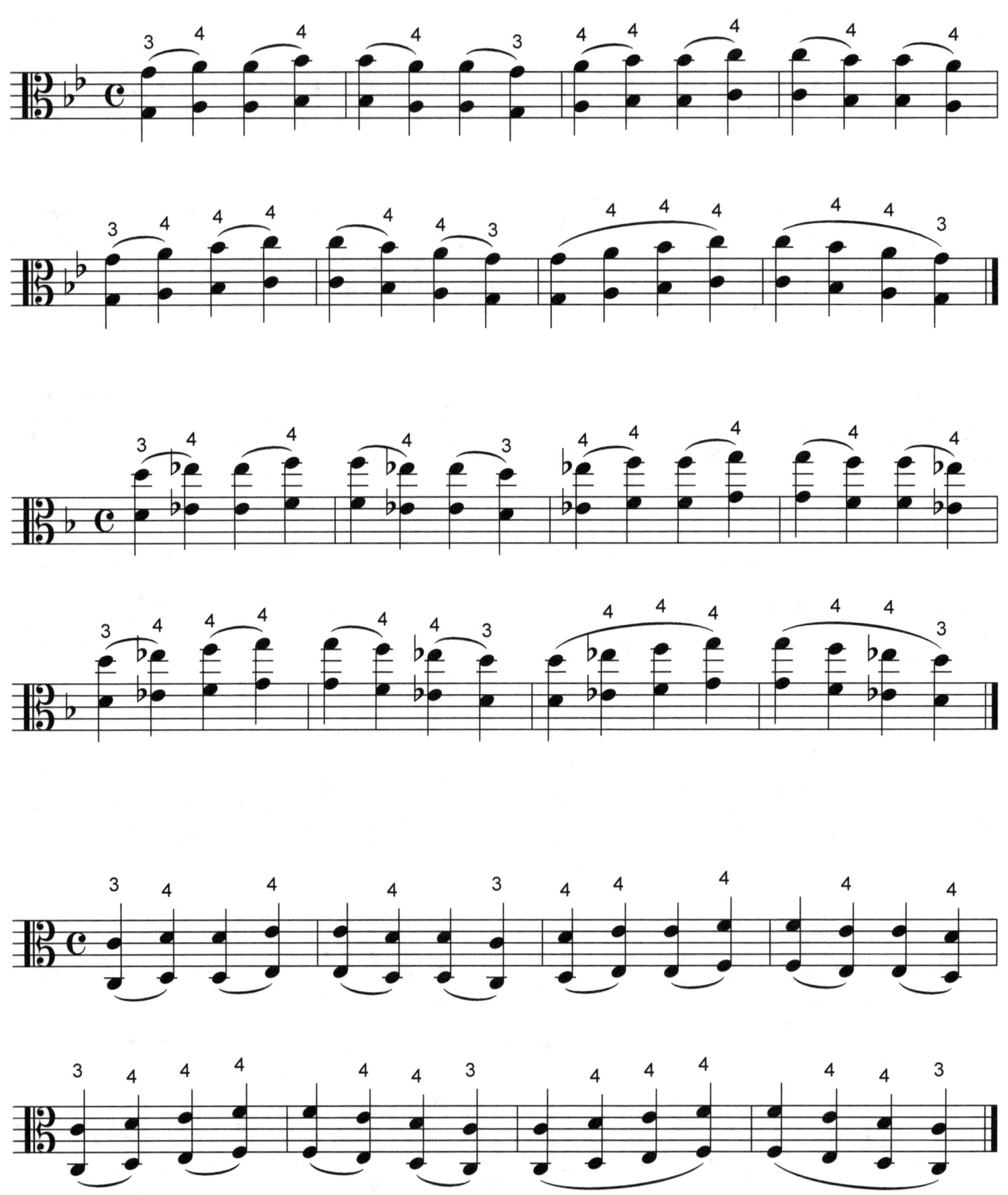

34

available from **www.charveypublications.com**: CHP270

Fourth Position for the Viola

by Cassia Harvey

A. First Shifting on the A String

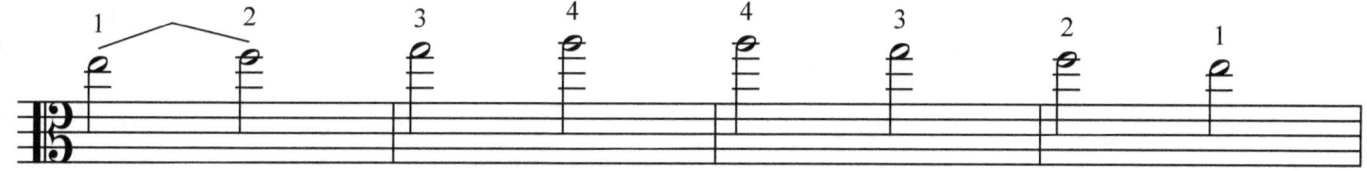

B. First Shifting on the D String

©2017 C. Harvey Publications All Rights Reserved.

www.ingramcontent.com/pod-product-compliance
Lightning Source LLC
Chambersburg PA
CBHW051427070526
44584CB00023B/3622